DATE DUE

OCT 3 0 1982		
FEB 1 9 1988		
MAR 4		
MAY 1 7 1990		
OCT 2 6 1990		
DEC 1 7 1990		

HIGHSMITH 45 220

Doctor Wotsit's Zoo!

By Felicia Law

Pictures by Esther Rowley

Gareth Stevens Publishing
Milwaukee

BRIGHT IDEA BOOKS:

First Words!
Picture Dictionary!
Opposites!
Sounds!

The Four Seasons!
Pets and Animal Friends!
The Age of Dinosaurs!
Baby Animals!

Doctor Wotsit's Zoo!
My Day at School!
Old Farm, New Farm!
Your Favorite Fairy Tales!

Mouse Count!
Time!
Animal ABC!
Animal 1*2*3!

Homes Then and Now!
Other People, Other Homes!

Dressing Up!
It's Fun to Cook!
Make It with Odds and Ends!

Space Trip!
Getting Around!
On Wheels!

Library of Congress Cataloging-in-Publication Data

Law, Felicia.
   Doctor Wotsit's zoo!

   (Bright idea books)

   Summary: Doctor Wotsit's tour of his zoo introduces the organization of zoos, the exotic and common species of animals kept there in their natural habitats, and the philosophy behind their preservation in such an environment.
   1. Zoos—Juvenile literature. 2. Zoo animals—Juvenile literature. (1. Zoos. 2. Zoo animals) I. Rowley, Esther, ill. II. Title.
QL76.L38   1986   590′.74′4   85-30439
ISBN 1-55532-048-1
ISBN 1-55532-023-6 (lib. bdg.)

This North American edition first published in 1986 by

Gareth Stevens, Inc.
7221 West Green Tree Road   Milwaukee, Wisconsin 53223, USA

U.S. edition, this format, copyright © 1986
Supplementary text copyright © 1986 by Gareth Stevens, Inc.
Illustrations copyright © 1984 by Octopus Books Limited

First published in the United Kingdom with an original text copyright by Octopus Books Limited.

Typeset by Ries Graphics ltd.
Series Editors: MaryLee Knowlton and Mark J. Sachner
Cover Design: Gary Moseley
Reading Consultant: Kathleen A. Brau

Contents

"I'm here, Grandpa," said Rusty, "ready to
start work."

Doctor Wotsit looked up from his map of the zoo.

"You're just in time, Rusty!" he said. "I never
needed an assistant more.

"Let's go! I'll give you a tour of the zoo. By the end of the day you'll know all about what we do here."

"Coming to the zoo makes me feel that I've seen the world," said Rusty. "The animals are from everywhere!"

"That's true, Rusty," said Doctor Wotsit. "And what's more important is that some animals are no longer in their original homes. Industry and cities and roads have changed their habitats. The animals may not be able to survive these changes.

"Take the Asiatic lion, Rusty. There are probably no more than two hundred of these fine creatures left in the world.

"My zoo cares for many animals who may soon die out, or become extinct. We try to breed more of these rare animals.

"To care for these animals, we must learn about them, Rusty. We start with finding out what they eat. Tell me, what did you eat when you were little?"

"Cheeseburgers, corn flakes, and rainbow sundaes!" said Rusty. "Just like now!"

"You're lucky we can ship things, Rusty!" laughed Doctor Wotsit. "Most animals must eat the food they find around them."

9

"You have much to learn, Rusty," Doctor Wotsit said seriously. "We all do. I'm going to invite all the children to visit the zoo to learn about animals. And the children will teach their parents. My zoo will be an educational center."

Rusty was beginning to think that being a zoo assistant was hard work. "Couldn't I just walk around and look at the animals?" he asked.

"Sorry, Rusty," his grandfather smiled. "*We're* here to work. We want to make this zoo a place for people of all ages to visit.

"Here people can stroll among the animals and admire their beautiful coats and markings and their strong, muscular movements.

"Here is the tropical house," said Doctor Wotsit. "Some of the animals have been brought here from much warmer countries. They need specially heated homes.

"The newborn baby animals may need special
attention in expensive incubators. When they are
fully grown we'll need more cages to house them.
A zoo is expensive to run, Rusty.

"Inside this strong concrete cage are two gorillas, a male and a female. The gorillas swing on the bars and rings that hang from the roof. They climb on the tubs and run up and down the slanted floor.

"In the forests, the gorillas get plenty of exercise as they search for food. Here, their food is found for them, but they still need exercise.

19

"This cage is for the chimpanzees. Smaller monkeys are even more active than big ones, Rusty. Be careful of your cap! They'll try to take it.

"Watch them grip the bars and swing along on their long arms. See how they use their tails to swing."

Rusty wanted to play with the chimpanzees. They seemed to have some good toys — balls, bats, rubber rings, and hoops. Rusty even saw a bicycle. They seemed just like people!

"Chimpanzees learn very fast because they like to copy human beings," said Doctor Wotsit.

RUFFED LEMUR

MADAGASCAR

Africa

LEMUR VARIEGATUS

Doctor Wotsit showed Rusty the cage of the ruffed lemur.

"The ruffed lemur comes from Madagascar, Rusty," said Doctor Wotsit. "And Lemur Variegatus is the Latin name of its family. Although the lemur lives in a big family group, it likes to have a place of its own."

"I do, too," said Rusty. "That's why I painted KEEP OUT. THIS MEANS YOU! on my door."

"The lemur manages without paint," said Doctor Wotsit. "See how the male is rubbing his scent along the branch. 'This is my territory,' he is saying. 'This is for me and my mate and our children.'"

Doctor Wotsit showed Rusty another animal who marks out his territory. "Many animals do this in the wild. They mark their zoo cages, too."

Rusty and Doctor Wotsit watched the bears. The male marched slowly around his enclosure. He always walked along the same trail.

"Doesn't he get bored walking around the same path all day?" asked Rusty.

"Sadly, Rusty, you may be right," answered Doctor Wotsit. "Animals in zoos are like guests in fancy hotels. Everything they need is brought to them.

"That is why the design of the cage is important. That is also why we take so much trouble finding a mate for each animal.

"Have you ever heard about the famous Giant Panda in the London Zoo? His name is Chi-Chi, and a mate was brought to him all the way from China. Everyone wanted to see a baby panda born, because only one has been born in captivity. But Chi-Chi was not interested, and the female panda went back to China."

27

Rusty enjoyed seeing the baby animals. Sometimes he couldn't find them because they stayed close to their mothers. They hid in their mothers' fur or curled up asleep inside their paws.

He spotted the baby kangaroo peeping out of its mother's pouch.

"If I had a pouch like that," teased Doctor Wotsit, "I would put you inside to keep you from getting lost, Rusty."

"I would enjoy that," said Rusty happily, "especially if you had strong back legs and could hop along the ground as fast as a kangaroo!"

"Time to do some work," said Doctor Wotsit. And he helped Rusty into a long coat. "Let's feed the seals in the pool."

Rusty held the fish high in the air, and the seals climbed onto the concrete, puffing and sniffing at the tasty smell. He threw the fish high in the air and the seals rose on their front flippers and neatly snapped up the food.

"It won't take long to feed the pelicans," said Doctor Wotsit. "They grab the food from the bucket if you're not looking."

The penguins waddled towards Rusty on their webbed feet. They flapped their little wings in protest when he tipped the bucket into the water. Now they would have to dive below the surface for their food.

30

Nearby the pelicans yawned and waited. Rusty threw the fish into their wide, gaping mouths.

They yawned for a second helping. Rusty yawned, too.

"Yawning is catching," said the Doctor. "Let's sit on the grass and eat our lunch."

"It's very peaceful here," said Rusty, as he relaxed on the grass. "Where are all the animals?"

"There are plenty of animals, Rusty, but you haven't noticed them," said the Doctor.

Rusty looked around. Something with stripes moved among the shadows of the bushes. "I think I see a tiger," said Rusty. "Yes, I do. No, I don't. Now I do. And now I don't!"

"The tiger's striped skin helps him hide in the jungle because the stripes look like shadows," said the Doctor. "That is called camouflage."

Later, Rusty learned about other animals who can disguise themselves against their background. "I almost stepped on that snake!" he cried in a terrified voice.

"No, you didn't," said the Doctor. "It moved away when it heard you coming. But I agree, it was hard to see against the sandy rocks.

"Here's another animal that camouflages itself,"
Doctor Wotsit said. "A chameleon changes color
depending on where it is resting. A neat trick, don't
you think, Rusty?"

Rusty and Doctor Wotsit drove the meat truck to the lions' enclosure.

"Are we safe?" Rusty asked. "There's no wire around the lions."

"Lions won't leap over this dry ditch," said Doctor Wotsit. "They like room to roam around, but they spend most of their time lying under the trees. Throw in the meat, Rusty. They can smell it now. Waiting upsets them."

Rusty learned that all the hunting cats are carnivores. He threw meat to the jaguars, the leopards, and the cheetahs. The puma did not move from his resting place in the fork of the tree.

"He must not be hungry, Rusty," said Doctor Wotsit. "Unlike us, these animals only eat when they are hungry. In the wild, they may go several days between one hunt and the next."

Rusty and Doctor Wotsit put on clean white coats, masks, and plastic gloves. They pushed open the door of the Quarantine Center, where animals stayed while they were being examined.

"This young raccoon arrived from a Maine forest last week," said Doctor Wotsit. "We'll keep it here for several weeks to check its health. If it is healthy, we'll let it join the other raccoons in the zoo.

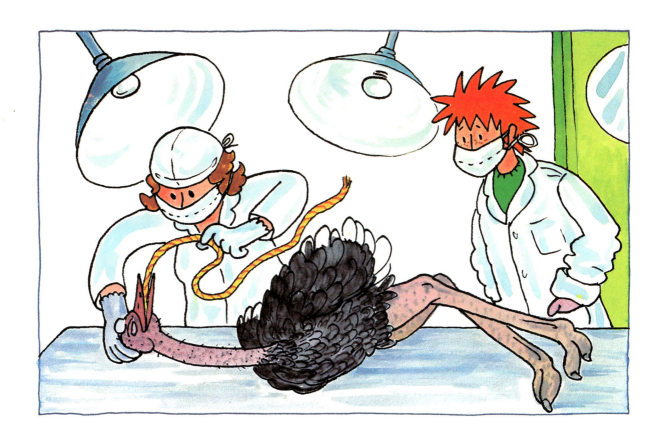

"Now pull the mask over your face, Rusty. We're going into the operating room."

Rusty saw a young ostrich stretched out in the operating room. It lay very still while the veterinarian pulled a plastic cord from its throat.

"Don't worry, Rusty," said the vet. "Once the anesthetic wears off, it will feel as good as new. I hope it won't pick up garbage that's thrown into its cage again."

"Your job will be to keep visitors from feeding the animals with their picnic scraps," said Doctor Wotsit.

"Why don't they read the signs?" asked Rusty.

"They do, Rusty, but they think they know better," said Doctor Wotsit sadly.

Rusty helped prepare the food for the animals in quarantine and in the animal hospital. He chopped the fruit and nuts for the marmosets. He soaked the pellets for the orangutan. He carefully weighed out the food and added a vitamin pill.

Rusty stared at the white-tailed sea eagle. The eagle stared back.

"I know," said Rusty. "I'm just another animal to you."

At the end of the day, Doctor Wotsit found Rusty staring into a mirror in his office. "I have been looking at animals all day," said Rusty. "I thought I'd look at what *they* see? Rusty — Homo sapiens!"

The following "Things to Talk About and Do," "Fun Facts About Animals," "New Zoo Words," and "More Books About Zoos" offer grown-ups suggestions for further activities and ideas for young readers of *Doctor Wotsit's Zoo!*

Things to Talk About and Do

1. At your zoo, look at the animals. What do they do that people do?

2. On pages 6 and 7, Doctor Wotsit tells Rusty that some animals may die out in their natural homes. Here are some animals besides the Asiatic Lion that face extinction:
   a. greater kudu
   b. harp seal
   c. reindeer
   d. snow leopard
   e. grizzly bear
   f. American bison
   g. jaguar
   h. koala
   i. grey whale

   How many of these animals have you heard of? Have you ever seen one? Choose one of these animals and use your library to find out as much as you can about it.

3. Go to the zoo. Choose an animal that interests you and find out how it lives in the wild. How is its zoo enclosure similar to the animal's natural habitat?

4. Write a short report about a day in the life of an animal in the zoo. Then compare it with how that animal's day would be if it were in the wild.

5. Here are some more things you can look for at the zoo:
   - What do the mother animals do to take care of their babies?
   - What kinds of games do you see the babies playing? Do the adults play, too?

Fun Facts About Animals

Here are some records held by animals:

1. Speed Records

Land animal — Cheetah, 84 miles per hour
Bird — Peregrine falcon, 217 miles per hour
Snake — Black mamba, 7 miles per hour
Fish — Swordfish, 56 miles per hour

2. Jumping Records

Kangaroo — 43 feet
Flea — 10 inches
Frog — 16 feet

3. Size Records

Largest fish — Whale shark, 66 feet
Smallest fish — Dwarf goby, .338 inch, full grown
Largest animal — Blue whale, 98 feet
Tallest land animal — Giraffe, 18 feet
Largest reptile — Salt water crocodile, 20 feet
Longest snake — Anaconda, 33 feet
Largest bird — Ostrich, 8 feet
Smallest bird — Bee hummingbird, 2 inches, $\frac{1}{10}$ ounce
Longest animal — Ribbon worm or Bootlace worm, 180 feet
Smallest animal — Bumblee bat, .062 (about $\frac{1}{20}$) inch

4. Miscellaneous Records

Slowest land mammal — Three-toed sloth, 6-8 feet per minute
Longest-lived animal — Tortoise, 152 years

New Zoo Words

camouflage . coloring that helps an animal blend in.
The frog's <u>camouflage</u> helps it hide in the grass.

captivity . . . . being confined or restrained.
Some animals do not have babies in a state of <u>captivity</u>.

disguise . . . . change the way something looks so it can hide.
A snake can <u>disguise</u> itself against sandy rocks.

enclosure . . . closed off space.
In some zoos, each <u>enclosure</u> is like a natural habitat.

extinct . . . . . no longer living anywhere in the world.
The dinosaur is now <u>extinct</u>.

habitat . . . . . living space.
The lion's natural <u>habitat</u> is the jungle.

muscular . . . physically strong and powerful.
The kangaroo has <u>muscular</u> back legs for jumping.

quarantine . . separate from other animals or people.
The veterinarian kept the sick llama in <u>quarantine</u>.

scent . . . . smell.
The <u>scent</u> of the lion warned the zebras to stay away.

territory . . . . . space.
The bear marked its <u>territory</u> by tramping down the grass.

More Books About Zoos

Here are some more books about zoos. Look at the list. If you see any books you would like to read, see if your library or bookstore has them.

Baby Animals! Thomson (Gareth Stevens)
Careers at a Zoo. Lerner (Lerner Publications)
Day in the Life of a Zoo Veterinarian. Paige (Troll)
Gumdrop at the Zoo. Biro (Gareth Stevens)
Koko's Kitten. Patterson (Scholastic Book Service)
Life in the Zoo. Chinery (Taplinger)
Pets and Animal Friends! Mitchell (Gareth Stevens)
Wild Orphan Babies: Mammals and Birds. Weber (Holt, Rinehart & Winston)
Wildlife in Danger. Burton (Silver Burdett)
Zoos in the Making. Shuttlesworth (Dutton)
Zoos Without Cages. Rinard (National Geographic)

For Grown-ups

Doctor Wotsit's Zoo! is a picture book with a factual text that introduces young readers to the philosophy and organization of zoos. As Doctor Wotsit shows Rusty, his new assistant, around the zoo, Rusty and the readers learn about both exotic and common species of animals and the need to preserve them. Readers also see how and why zoos try to reproduce the natural habitats of animals.

The editors invite interested adults to examine the sampling of reading level estimates below. While reading level estimates help adults decide what reading materials are appropriate for children at certain grade levels, they are nonetheless only estimates.

Most reading specialists agree that efforts to encourage young readers should be based not only on reading level estimates but on practice in reading, listening, speaking, and drawing meaning from language. These activities, which encourage young readers to use language beyond the scope of the text, are developed in the supplementary sections of *Doctor Wotsit's Zoo!* These activities also give adults a chance to participate in the learning — and fun — to be found in this story.

Reading level analysis: SPACHE 2.6, FRY 2.5, FLESCH 87 (easy), RAYGOR 3.5, FOG 6, SMOG 3